POETRY FROM CRESCENT MOON

Edmund Spenser: *Heavenly Love: Selected Poems*
selected and introduced by Teresa Page

Edmund Spenser: *Amoretti*
edited by Teresa Page

Robert Herrick: *Delight In Disorder: Selected Poems*
edited and introduced by M.K. Pace

Sir Thomas Wyatt: *Love For Love: Selected Poems*
selected and introduced by Louise Cooper

John Donne: *Air and Angels: Selected Poems*
selected and introduced by A.H. Ninham

D.H. Lawrence: *Being Alive: Selected Poems*
edited with an introduction by Margaret Elvy

D.H. Lawrence: Symbolic Landscapes
by Jane Foster

D.H. Lawrence: Infinite Sensual Violence
by M.K. Pace

Percy Bysshe Shelley: *Paradise of Golden Lights: Selected Poems*
selected and introduced by Charlotte Greene

Thomas Hardy: *Her Haunting Ground: Selected Poems*
edited, with an introduction by A.H. Ninham

Sexing Hardy: Thomas Hardy and Feminism
by Margaret Elvy

Emily Bronte: *Darkness and Glory: Selected Poems*
selected and introduced by Miriam Chalk

John Keats: *Bright Star: Selected Poems*
edited with an introduction by Miriam Chalk

John Keats: *Poems of 1820*
edited with an introduction by Miriam Chalk

Henry Vaughan: *A Great Ring of Pure and Endless Light: Selected Poems*
selected and introduced by A.H. Ninham

The Crescent Moon Book of Love Poetry
edited by Louise Cooper

The Crescent Moon Book of Mystical Poetry in English
edited by Carol Appleby

The Crescent Moon Book of Nature Poetry From Langland to Lawrence
edited by Margaret Elvy

The Crescent Moon Book of Metaphysical Poetry
edited and introduced by Charlotte Greene

The Crescent Moon Book of Elizabethan Love Poetry
edited and introduced by Carol Appleby

The Crescent Moon Book of Romantic Poetry
edited and introduced by L.M. Poole

Peter Redgrove: Here Comes the Flood
by Jeremy Mark Robinson

Sex-Magic-Poetry-Cornwall: A Flood of Poems
by Peter Redgrove, edited with an essay by Jeremy Mark Robinson

Brigitte's Blue Heart
by Jeremy Reed

Claudia Schiffer's Red Shoes
by Jeremy Reed

By-Blows: Uncollected Poems
by D.J. Enright

Petrarch, Dante and the Troubadours: The Religion of Love and Poetry
by Cassidy Hughes

Dante: *Selections From the Vita Nuova*
translated by Thomas Okey

Arthur Rimbaud: *Selected Poems*
edited and translated by Andrew Jary

Arthur Rimbaud: *A Season in Hell*
edited and translated by Andrew Jary

Friedrich Hölderlin: *Hölderlin's Songs of Light: Selected Poems*
translated by Michael Hamburger

SELECTED POEMS

Selected Poems

William Shakespeare

Edited by Mark Tuley

CRESCENT MOON

First published 1994. Revised 2020.
Introduction and Notes © Mark Tuley 1994, 2020.

Printed and bound in the U.S.A.
Set in Garamond Book 12 on 18pt.
Designed by Radiance Graphics.

The right of Mark Tuley to be identified as the editor of this book has been
asserted generally in accordance with sections 77 and 78 of the Copyright,
Designs and Patents Act 1988.

British Library Cataloguing in Publication data available

ISBN-13 9781861717795

CRESCENT MOON PUBLISHING
P.O. Box 1312, Maidstone
Kent, ME14 5XU
Great Britain
www.crmoon.com

CONTENTS

William Shakespeare

SHAKE-SPEARES

SONNETS.

Neuer before Imprinted.

AT LONDON
By G. Eld for T. T. and are
to be solde by William Aspley.
1609.

TO. THE. ONLIE. BEGETTER. OF.
THESE. INSVING. SONNETS.
M'. W. H. ALL. HAPPINESSE.
AND. THAT. ETERNITIE.
PROMISED.

BY.

OVR. EVER-LIVING. POET.

WISHETH.

THE. WELL-WISHING.
ADVENTVRER. IN.
SETTING.
FORTH.

T. T.

SONNETS

❖

5

Those hours that with gentle work did frame
The lovely gaze where every eye doth dwell
Will play the tyrants to the very same,
And that unfair which fairly doth excel:
For never-resting time leads summer on
To hideous winter and confounds him there,
Sap cheek'd with frost, and lusty leaves quite gone,
Beauty o'versnow'd and bareness everywhere:
Then were not summer's distillation left
A liquid prisoner pent in walls of glass,
Beauty's effect with beauty were bereft,
Nor it nor no remembrance what it was.
    But flowers distill'd, though they with winter
                             meet,
    Leese but their show: their substance still lives
                             sweet.

18

Shall I compare thee to a summer's day?
Thou art more lovely and more temperate:
Rough winds do shake the darling buds of May,
And summer's lease hath all too short a date:
Sometimes too hot the eye of heaven shines,
And often is his gold complexion dimm'd,
And every fair from fair sometime declines,
By chance or nature's changing course untrimm'd:
But thy eternal summer shall not fade
Nor lose possession of that fair thou ow'st,
Nor shall Death brag thou wander'st in his shade,
When in eternal lines to time thou grow'st:
   So long as men can breathe or eyes can see,
   So long lives this, and this gives life to thee.

20

A woman's face with nature's own hand painted
Hast thou, the master-mistress of my passion;
A woman's gentle heart, but not acquainted
With shifting change as is false women's fashion;
An eye more bright than theirs, less false in rolling,
Gilding the object whereupon it gazeth;
A man in hue all hues in so controlling,
Which steals men's eyes and women's souls amazeth:
And for a woman wert thou first created, –
Till nature as she wrought thee fell a-doting,
And by addition me of thee defeated,
By adding one thing to my purpose nothing.
    But since she prick'd thee out for women's
                          pleasure,
    Mine be thy love and thy love's use their pleasure.

33

Full many a glorious morning have I seen
Flatter the mountain tops with sovereign eye,
Kissing with golden face the meadows green,
Gilding pale streams with heavenly alchemy, –
Anon permit the basest clouds to ride
With ugly rack on his celestial face,
And from the forlorn world his visage hide,
Stealing unseen to west with this disgrace:
Even so my sun one early morn did shine
With all triumphant splendour on my brow;
But out alack, he was but one hour mine –
The region cloud hath mask'd him from me now.
    Yet him for this my love no whit disdaineth:
    Suns of the world may stain, when heaven's sun
                       staineth.

36

Let me confess that we two must be twain
Although our undivided loves are one:
So shall those blots that do with me remain
Without thy help by me be borne alone.
In our two loves there is but one respect,
Though in our lives a separable spite,
Which, though it alter not love's sole effect,
Yet doth it steal sweet hours from love's delight.
I may not evermore acknowledge thee,
Lest my bewailed guilt should do thee shame;
Nor thou with public kindness honour me,
Unless thou take that honour from thy name:
    But do not so; I love thee in such sort
    As, thou being mine, mine is thy good report.

40

Take all my loves, my love, yea, take them all:
What hast thou then more than thou hadst before?
No love, my love, that thou mayst true love call –
All mine was thine, before thou hadst this more.
Then if for my love thou my love receivest,
I cannot blame thee, for my love thou usest, –
But yet be blam'd, if thou this self deceivest
By wilful taste of what thy self refusest.
I do forgive thy robbery, gentle thief,
Although thou steal thee all my poverty:
And yet love knows it is a greater grief
To bear love's wrong than hate's knowing injury.
    Lascivious grave, in whom all ill well shows,
    Kill me with spites, yet we must not be foes.

54

Oh how much more doth beauty beauteous seem
By that sweet ornament which truth doth give!
The rose looks fair, but fairer we it deem
For that sweet odour which doth in it live.
The canker blooms have full as deep a dye
As the perfumed tincture of the roses,
Hang on such thorns and play as wantonly
When summer's breath their masked buds discloses:
But for their virtue only is their show
They live unwoo'd and unrespected fade –
Die to themselves. Sweet roses do not so;
Of their sweet deaths are sweetest odours made:
     And so of you, beauteous and lovely youth,
     When that shall fade, by verse distils your truth.

56

Sweet love, renew thy force; be it not said
Thy edge should blunter be than appetite,
Which but today by feeding is allay'd,
Tomorrow sharpen'd in his former might:
So, love, be thou; although today thou fill
Thy hungry eyes even till they wink with fulness,
Tomorrow see again, and do not kill
The spirit of love with a perpetual dulness:
Let this sad interim like the ocean be
Which parts the shore where two contracted new
Come daily to the banks, that when they see
Return of love more blest may be the view:
    As call it winter, which being full of care
    Makes summer's welcome, thrice more wish'd,
                      more rare.

57

Being your slave, what should I do but tend
Upon the hours and times of your desire?
I have no precious time at all to spend,
Nor services to do, till you require:
Nor dare I chide the world-without-end hour
Whilst I, my sovereign, watch the clock for you,
Nor think the bitterness of absence sour
When you have bid your servant once adieu:
Nor dare I question with my jealous thought
Where you may be, or your affairs suppose,
But like a sad slave stay and think of nought
Save where you are how happy you make those.
   So true a fool is love that in your will,
   Though you do anything, he thinks no ill.

73

That time of year thou mayst in me behold
When yellow leaves, or none, or few, do hang
Upon those boughs which shake against the cold,
Bare ruin'd choirs where late the sweet birds sang:
In me thou see'st the twilight of such day
As after sunset fadeth in the west,
Which by and by black night doth take away,
Death's second self that seals up all in rest:
In me thou see'st the glowing of such fire
That on the ashes of his youth doth lie
As the death-bed whereon it must expire,
Consum'd with that which it was nourish'd by:
   This thou perceiv'st, which makes thy love more
                    strong
   To love that well which thou must leave ere long.

76

Why is my verse so barren of new pride,
So far from variation or quick change?
Why with the time do I not glance aside
To new-found methods and to compounds strange?
Why write I still all one, ever the same,
And keep invention in a moted weed,
That every word doth almost tell my name,
Shewing their birth and where they did proceed?
Oh know, sweet love, I always write of you,
And you and love are still my argument;
So all my best is dressing old words new,
Spending again what is already spent:
    For as the sun is daily new and old,
    So is my love still telling what is told.

97

How like a winter hath my absence been
From thee, the pleasure of the fleeting year!
What freezings have I felt, what dark days seen! –
What old December's bareness everywhere!
And yet this time remov'd was summer's time, –
The teeming autumn big with rich increase
Bearing the wanton burthen of the prime,
Like widow'd wombs after their lords' decrease:
Yet this abundant issue seem'd to me
But hope of orphans, and unfather'd fruit;
For summer and his pleasures wait on thee,
And thou away the very birds are mute:
    Or if they sing, 'tis with so dull a cheer
    That leaves look pale, dreading the winter's near.

104

To me, fair friend, you can never be old,
For as you were when first your eye I eyed
Such seems your beauty still: three winters cold
Have from the forests shook three summer's pride,
Three beauteous springs to yellow autumn turn'd
In process of the seasons have I seen,
Three April perfumes in three hot Junes burn'd,
Since first I saw you fresh which yet are green.
Ah yet doth beauty like a dial hand
Steal from his figure and no pace perceiv'd,
So your sweet hue, which methinks still doth stand,
Hath motion, and mine eye may be deceiv'd,
    For fear of which hear this, thou age unbred:
    Ere you were born was beauty's summer dead.

116

Let me not to the marriage of true minds
Admit impediments: love is not love
Which alters when it alteration finds,
Or bends with the remover to remove.
Oh no! it is an ever-fixed mark
That looks on tempests and is never shaken;
It is the star to every wandering bark,
Whose worth's unknown although his height be taken.
Love's not Time's fool, though rosy lips and cheeks
Within his bending sickle's compass come;
Love alters not with his brief hours and weeks,
But bears it out even to the edge of doom.
    If this be error and upon me prov'd,
    I never writ, nor no man ever lov'd.

129

The expense of spirit in a waste of shame
Is lust in action; and till action, lust
Is perjur'd, murderous, bloody, full of blame,
Savage, extreme, rude, cruel, not to trust;
Enjoy'd no sooner but despised straight;
Past reason hunted; and no sooner had,
Past reason hated, as a swallow'd bait
On purpose laid to make the taker mad, –
Mad in pursuit, and in possession so;
Had, having, and in quest to have, extreme;
A bliss in proof; and prov'd, a very woe;
Before, a joy propos'd; behind, a dream.
    All this the world well knows; yet none knows well
    To shun the heaven that leads men to this hell.

130

My mistress' eyes are nothing like the sun;
Coral is far more red than her lips' red;
If snow be white, why then her breasts are dun;
If hairs be wires, black wires grown on her head:
I have seen roses damask'd, red and white,
But no such roses see I in her cheeks;
And in some perfumes is there more delight
Than in the breath that from my mistress reeks:
I love to hear her speak, yet well I know
That music hath a far more pleasing sound;
I grant I never saw a goddess go, –
My mistress when she walks treads on the ground.
   And yet by heaven when I think my love as rare
   As any she belied with false compare.

147

My love is as a fever, longing still
For that which longer nurseth the disease,
Feeding on that which doth preserve the ill,
The uncertain sickly appetite to please.
My reason, the physician to my love,
Angry that his prescriptions are not kept,
Hath left me, and I desperate now approve
Desire is death, which physic did except.
Past cure I am now reason is past care,
And frantic mad with evermore unrest;
My thoughts and my discourse as madmen's are,
At random from the truth, vainly express'd:
    For I have sworn thee fair, and thought thee bright,
    Who art black as hell, as dark as night.

152

In loving thee thou know'st I am forsworn;
But thou art twice forsworn to me love swearing, –
In act thy bed-vow broke, and new faith torn
In vowing new hate, after new love bearing.
But why of two oath's breach do I accuse thee,
When I break twenty? I am perjur'd most:
For all my vows are oaths but to misuse thee,
And all my honest faith in thee is lost.
For I have sworn deep oaths of thy deep kindness –
Oaths of thy love, thy truth, thy constancy;
And to enlighten thee gave eyes to blindness,
Or made them swear against the thing they see:
    For I have sworn thee fair, – more perjur'd eye,
    To swear against the truth so foul a lie!

POEMS

✤

❖

The Phoenix and Turtle

Let the bird of loudest lay,
On the sole Arabian tree,
Herald sad and trumpet be,
To whose sound chaste wings obey.

But thou, shrieking harbinger,
Foul pre-currer of the fiend,
Augur of the fever's end,
To this troop come thou not near.

From this session interdict
Every fowl of tyrant wing,
Save the eagle, feather'd king:
Keep the obsequy so strict.

Let the priest in surplice white,
That defunctive music can,
Be the death-defying swan,
Lest the requiem lack his right.

And thou, treble-dated crow,
That thy sable gender mak'st
With the breath thou giv'st and tak'st,
'mongst our mourners shalt thou go.

Here the anthem doth commence:
Love and constancy is dead;
Phoenix and the turtle fled

In a mutual flame from hence.

So they lov'd, as love in twain
Had the essence but in one;
Two distincts, division none:
Number there in love was slain.

Hearts remote, yet not asunder;
Distance, and no space was seen
'Twixt the turtle and his queen;
But in them it were a wonder.

So between them love did shine,
That the turtle saw his right
Flaming in the phoenix' sight:
Either was the other's mine.

Property was thus appall'd,
That the self was not the same;
Single nature's double name
Neither two nor one was call'd.

Reason, in itself confounded,
Saw division grow together;
To themselves yet either-neither,
Simple were so well compounded.

That it cried how true a twain
Seemeth this concordant one!
Love hath reason, reason none
If what parts can so remain.

Whereupon it made this threne
To the phoenix and the dove,
Co-supreme and stars of love;

As chorus to their tragic scene.

✤

THRENOS

Beauty, truth, and rarity.
Grace in all simplicity,
Here enclos'd in cinders lie.

Death is now the phoenix' nest;
And the turtle's loyal breast
To eternity doth rest,

Leaving no posterity:-
'Twas not their infirmity,
It was married chastity.

Truth may seem, but cannot be:
Beauty brag, but 'tis not she;
Truth and beauty buried be.

To this urn let those repair
That are either true or fair;
For these dead birds sigh a prayer.

II

Two loves I have, of comfort and despair,
That like two spirits do suggest me still;
My better angel is a man right fair,
My worser spirit a woman colour'd ill.
To win me soon to hell, my female evil
Tempteth my better angel from my side,
And would corrupt my saint to be a devil,
Wooing his purity with her fair pride.
And whether that my angel be turn'd fiend,
Suspect I may, yet not directly tell:
For being both to me, both to each friend,
I guess one angel in another's hell;
    The truth I shall not know, but live in doubt,
    Till my bad angel fire my good one out.

VII

Fair is my love, but not so fair as fickle;
Mild as a dove, not neither true nor trusty;
Brighter than glass, and yet, as glass is, brittle;
Softer than wax, and yet, as iron, rusty;
    A lily pale, with damask dye to grace her;
    None fairer, nor none falser to deface her.

Her lips to mine how often hath she joined,
Between each kiss her oaths of true love swearing!
How many tales to please me hath she coined,
Dreading my love, the loss whereof still fearing!
    Yet, in the midst of all her pure protestings,
    Her faith, her oaths, her tears, and all, were jestings.

She burn'd with love, as straw with fire flameth,

She burn'd out love, as soon as straw out-burneth;
She fram'd the love, and yet she foil'd the framing,
She bade love last, and yet she fell a-turning.
    Was this a lover, or a lecher whether?
    Bad in the best, though excellent in neither.

VIII

If music and sweet poetry agree,
As they must needs, the sister and the brother,
Then must the love be great 'twixt thee and me,
Because thou lovest the one, and I the other.
Dowland to thee is dear, whose heavenly touch
Upon the lute doth ravish human sense;
Spenser to me, whose deep conceit is such
As, passing all conceit, needs no defence.
Thou lovest to hear the sweet melodious sound
That Phoebus' lute, the queen of music, makes;
And I in deep delight am chiefly drown'd
When as himself to singing he betakes.
    One god is god of both, as poets feign;
    One knight loves both, and both in thee remain.

XX

Live with me, and be my love,
And we will all the pleasures prove
That hills and valleys, dales and fields,
And all the craggy mountains yields.

There will we sit upon the rocks,
And see the shepherds feed their flocks,
By shallow rivers, by whose falls

Melodious birds sing madrigals.

There will I make thee a bed of roses,
With a thousand fragrant posies,
A cap of flowers, and a kirtle
Embroider'd all with leaves of myrtle.

A belt of straw and ivy buds,
With coral clasps and amber studs;
And if these pleasures may thee move,
Then live with me and be my love.

LOVE'S ANSWER

If that the world and love were young,
And truth in every shepherd's tongue,
These pretty pleasures might me move
To live with thee and be thy love.

from *The Passionate Pilgrim*

✤

This said, impatience chokes her pleading tongue,
And swelling passion doth provoke a pause;
Red cheeks and fiery eyes blaze forth he wrong;
Being judge in love, she cannot right her cause:
    And now she weeps, and now she fain would speak,
    And now her sobs do her intendments break.

Sometimes she shakes her head and then his hand,
Now gazeth she on him, now on the ground;
Sometimes her arms infold him like a band:
She would, he will not in her arms be bound;
    And when from thence he struggles to be gone,
    She locks her lily fingers one in one.

'Fondling,' she saith, 'since I have hemm'd thee here
Within the circuit of this ivory pale,
I'll be a park, and thou shalt be my deer;
Feed where thou wilt, on mountain or in dale:
    Graze on my lips; and if those hills be dry,
    Stray lower, where the pleasant fountains lie.

Within this limit is relief enough,
Sweet bottom-grass and high delightful plain,
Round rising hillocks, brakes obscure and rough,
To shelter thee from tempest and from rain
    Then be my deer, since I am such a park;
    No dog shall rouse thee, though a thousand bark.'

At this Adonis smiles as in disdain,
That in each cheek appears a pretty dimple:
Love made those hollows, if himself were slain,
He might be buried in a tomb so simple;

Foreknowing well, if there he came to lie,
Why, there Love lived and there he could not die.

These lovely caves, these round enchanting pits,
Open'd their mouths to swallow Venus' liking.
Being mad before, how doth she now for wits?
Struck dead at first, what needs a second striking?
    Poor queen of love, in thine own law forlorn,
    To love a cheek that smiles at thee in scorn!

Now which way shall she turn? what shall she say?
Her words are done, her woes are more increasing;
The time is spent, her object will away,
And from her twining arms doth urge releasing.
    'Pity,' she cries, 'some favour, some remorse!'
    Away he springs and hasteth to his horse.

Venus. *Venus and Adonis, 217-258*

PLAYS

❧

✣

But love, first learned in a lady's eyes,
Lives not alone immured in the brain,
But with the motion of all elements
Courses as swift as thought in every power,
And gives to every power a double power,
Above their functions and their offices.
It adds a precious seeing to the eye:
A lover's eyes will gaze an eagle blind.
A lover's ear will hear the lowest sound,
When the suspicious head of theft is stopp'd.
Love's feeling is more soft and sensible
Than are the tender horns of cockled snails;
Love's tongue proves dainty Bacchus gross in taste.
For valour, is not Love a Hercules,
Still climbing trees in the Hesperides?
Subtle as Sphinx; as sweet and musical
As bright Apollo's lute, strung with his hair.
And when Love speaks, the voice of all the gods
Make heaven drowsy with the harmony.
Never durst poet touch a pen to write
Until his ink were temp'red with love's sighs;
O, then his lines would ravish savage ears,
And plant in tyrants mild humility.
From women's eyes this doctrine I derive.
They sparkle still the right Promethean fire;
They are the books, the arts, the academes,
That show, contain, and nourish, all the world,
Else none at all in aught proves excellent.

Berowne. *Love's Labour's Lost*, 4.3.323-350

✣

O mistress mine, where are you roaming?
O, stay and hear; your true love's coming,
   That can sing both high and low.
   Trip no further, pretty sweeting;
   Journeys end in lovers meeting,
   Every wise man's son doth know.

What is love? 'Tis not hereafter;
Present mirth hath present laughter;
   What's to come is still unsure.
   In delay there lies no plenty,
   Then come kiss me, sweet and twenty;
   Youth's stuff will not endure.

Clown. *Twelfth Night,* 2.3.38-51

❧

I would I had some flowers o' the spring that might
Become your time of day; and yours, and yours,
That wear upon your virgin branches yet
Your maidenheads growing: O Prosperina!
For the flowers now that frighted me thou let'st fall
From Dis's waggon! – daffodils,
That come before the swallow dares, and take
The winds of March with beauty; violets, dim
But sweeter than the lids of Juno's eyes
Or Cytherea's breath; pale primroses,
That die unmarried ere they can behold
Bright Phoebus in his strength – a malady
Most incident to maids; bold oxlips, and
The crown-imperial; lilies of all kinds,
The flow'r-de-luce being one. O, these I lack
To make you garlands of, and my sweet friend
To strew him him o'er and o'er!

Perdita. *The Winter's Tale, 4.4.113-128*

❖

I am giddy; expectation whirls me round.
Th' imaginary relish is so sweet
That it enchants my sense; what will it be
When that the wat'ry palate tastes indeed
Love's thrice-repured nectar? Death, I fear me;
Swooning destruction; or some joy too fine,
Too subtle-potent, tun'd too sharp in sweetness,
For the capacity of my ruder powers.
I fear it much; and I do fear besides
That I shall lose distinction in my joys;
As doth a battle, when they charge on heaps
The enemy flying.

Troilus. *Troilus and Cressida*, 3.2.16-28

❖

When she first met Mark Anthony she purs'd up his
heart, upon the river of Cydnus.
There she appear'd indeed! Or my reporter devis'd
well for her. I will tell you.
The barge she sat in, like a burnish'd throne,
Burn'd on the water. The poop was beaten gold;
Purple the sails, and so perfumed that
The winds were love-sick with them; the oars were
                                            silver,
Which to the tune of flutes kept stroke, and made
The water which they beat to follow faster,
As amorous of their strokes. For her own person,
It beggar'd description. She did lie
In her pavilion, cloth-of-gold, of tissue,
O'erpicturing that Venus where we see
The fancy out-work nature. On each side her
Stood pretty dimpled boys, like smiling Cupids,
With divers-colour'd fans, whose wind did seem
To glow the delicate cheeks which they did cool,
And what they undid did.
Her gentlewomen, like the Nereides,
So many mermaids, tended her i' th' eyes,
And made their ends adornings. At the helm
A seeming mermaid steers. The silken tackle
Swell with the touches of those flower-soft hands
That yarely frame the office. From the barge
A strange invisible perfume hits the sense
Of the adjacent wharfs. The city cast
Her people out upon her; and Antony,
Enthron'd i' th' market-place, did sit alone,
Whistling to th' air; which, but for vacancy,
Had gone to gaze on Cleopatra too,

And made a gap in nature.
Upon her landing, Antony sent to her,
Invited her to supper. She replied
It should be better he became her guest;
Which she entreated. Our courteous Antony,
Whom ne'er the word of 'No' woman heard speak,
Being barber'd ten times o'er, goes to the feast,
And for his ordinary pays his heart
For what his eyes eat only.

Enobarbus. *Antony and Cleopatra*, 2.2.195-229

❖

Gallop apace, you fiery-footed steeds
Towards Phoebus' lodging; such a waggoner
As Phaethon would whip you to the west,
And bring in cloudy night immediately.
Spread thy close curtain, love-performing night,
That runaways' eyes may wink, and Romeo
Leap to these arms, untalk'd of and unseen.
Lovers can see to do their amorous rites
By their own beauties; or if love be blind,
It best agrees with night. Come, civil night,
Thou sober-suited matron, all in black,
And learn me how to lose a winning match,
Play'd for a pair of stainless maidenhoods;
Hood my unmann'd blood, bating in my cheeks,
With thy black mantle, till strange love, grown bold,
Think true love acted simple modesty.
Come, night; come, Romeo; come, thou day in night;
For thou wilt lie upon the wings of night
Whiter than new snow on a raven's back.
Come, gentle night, come, loving black-brow'd night,
Give me my Romeo; and, when he shall die,
Take him and cut him out in little stars,
And he will make the face of heaven so fine
That all the world will be in love with night,
And pay no worship to the garish sun.

Juliet. *Romeo and Juliet*, 3.1.1-25

❖

Come, you spirits
That tend on mortal thoughts, unsex me here;
And fill me, from the crown to the toe, top-full
Of direst cruelty. Make thick my blood,
Stop up th' access and passage to remorse,
That no compunctious visitings of nature
Shake my fell purpose nor keep peace between
Th' effect and it. Come to my woman's breasts,
And take my milk for gall, you murd'ring ministers,
Wherever in your sightless substances
You wait on nature's mischief. Come, thick night,
And pall thee in the dunnest smoke of hell,
That my keen knife see not the wound it makes,
Nor heaven peep through the blanket of the dark
To cry 'Hold, hold'.

Lady Macbeth. *Macbeth*, 1.4.35-51

❖

Now the hungry lion roars,
And the wolf behowls the moon;
Whilst the heavy ploughman snores,
All with the weary task fordone.
Now the wasted brands do glow,
Whilst the screech-owl, screeching loud,
Puts the wretch that lies in woe
In remembrance of a shroud.
Now it is the time of night
That the graves, all gaping wide,
Every one lets forth his sprite,
In the church-way paths to glide.
And we fairies, that do run
By the triple Hecate's team
From the presence of the sun,
Following darkness like a dream,
Now are frolic.

Puck. *A Midsummer Night's Dream*, 5.1.360-376

❖

Be not afeard. The isle is full of noises,
Sounds, and sweet airs, that give delight, and hurt not.
Sometimes a thousand twangling instruments
Will hum about mine ears; and sometime voices,
That, if I then had wak'd after long sleep,
Will make me sleep again; and then, in dreaming,
The clouds methought would open and show riches
Ready to drop upon me, that, when I wak'd,
I cried to dream again.

Caliban. *The Tempest*, 3.2.130-138

❖

Blow, winds, and crack your cheeks; rage, blow.
You cataracts and hurricanoes, spout
Till you have drench'd our steeples, drown'd the cocks.
You sulph'rous and thought-executing fires,
Vaunt-couriers of oak-chewing thunder-bolts,
Singe my white head. And thou, all-shaking thunder,
Strike flat the thick rotundity o' th' world;
Crack nature's moulds, all germens spill at once,
That makes ingrateful man.
[…]
Rumble thy bellyful. Spit, fire; spout, rain.
Nor rain, wind, thunder, fire, are my daughters.
I tax not your elements, with unkindness;
I never gave you kingdom, call'd you children;
You owe me no subscription. Then let fall
Your horrible pleasure. Here I stand, your slave,
A poor, infirm, weak and despis'd old man;
But yet I call you servile ministers
That will with two pernicious daughters join
Your high-engender'd battles 'gainst a head
So old and white as this. O ho! 'tis foul!

Lear. *King Lear*, 3.2.1-9, 14-25

❖

Ye elves of hills, brooks, standing lakes, and groves;
And ye that on the sands with printless foot
Do chase the ebbing Neptune, and do fly him
When he comes back; you demi-puppets that
By moonshine do the green sour ringlets make,
Whereof the ewe not bites; and you whose pastime
Is to make midnight mushrooms, that rejoice
To hear the solemn curfew; by whose aid –
Weak masters though ye be – I have bedimm'd
The noontide sun, call'd forth the mutinous winds,
And 'twixt the green sea and the azur'd vault
Set roaring war. To the dread rattling thunder
Have I given fire, and rifted Jove's stout oak
With his own bolt; the strong-bas'd promontory
Have I made shake, and by the spurs pluck'd up
The pine and cedar. Graves at my command
Have wak'd their sleepers, op'd, and let 'em forth,
By my so potent art. But this rough magic
I here abjure; and, when I have requir'd
Some heavenly music – which even now I do –
To work mine end upon their senses that
This airy charm is for, I'll break my staff,
Bury it certain fathoms in the earth,
And deeper than did ever plummet sound
I'll drown my book.

Prospero. *The Tempest*, 5.1.33-57

❖

I have of late – but wherefore I know not – lost all
my mirth, forgone all custom of exercises; and
indeed it goes so heavily with my disposition that
this goodly frame, the earth, seems to me a sterile
promontory; this most excellent canopy the air,
look you, this brave o'er-hanging firmament, this
majestical roof fretted with golden fire – why, it
appeareth no other thing to me than a foul and
pestilent congregation of vapours. What a piece of
work is a man! how noble in reason! how infinite
in faculties! in form and moving, how express and
admirable! in action, how like an angel! in
apprehension, how like a god! the beauty of the
world! the paragon of animals! And yet, to me,
what is this quintessence of dust? Man delights not
me – no, nor woman neither, though by your
smiling you seem to say so.

Hamlet. *Hamlet,* 2.2.292-309

❖

To-morrow, and to-morrow, and to-morrow,
Creeps in this petty place from day to day,
To the last syllable of recorded time;
And all our yesterdays have lighted fools
The way to dusty death. Out, out, brief candle!
Life's but a walking shadow, a poor player
That struts and frets his hour upon the stage,
And then is heard no more: it is a tale
Told by an idiot, full of sound and fury,
Signifying nothing.

Macbeth. *Macbeth*, 5.5.19-28

❖

Now my charms are all o'erthrown,
And what strength I have's mine own,
Which is most faint. Now 'tis true,
I must be here confin'd by you,
Or sent to Naples. Let me not,
Since I have my dukedom got,
And pardon'd the deceiver, dwell
In this bare island by your spell;
But release me from my bands
With the help of your good hands.
Gentle breath of yours my sails
Must fill, or else my project fails,
Which was to please. Now I want
Spirits to enforce, art to enchant;
And my ending is despair
Unless I be reliev'd by prayer,
Which pierces so that it assaults
Mercy itself, and frees all faults.
As you from crimes would pardon'd be,
Let your indulgence set me free.

Prospero. *The Tempest*, Epilogue

♣

Our revels now are ended. These our actors,
As I foretold you, were all spirits, and
Are melted into air, into thin air;
And, like the baseless fabric of this vision,
The cloud-capp'd towers, the gorgeous palaces,
The solemn temples, the great globe itself,
Yea, all which it inherit, shall dissolve,
And, like this insubstantial pageant faded,
Leave not a rack behind. We are such stuff
As dreams are made on; and our little life
Is rounded with a sleep.

Prospero. *The Tempest*, 4.1.148-158

William Page, William Shakespeare, 1873

Eric Gill, portrait of Shakespeare, 1936

Shakespeare by Élisée Reclus (1830-1905)

Thomas Sully, William Shakespeare, 1864

And sue a friend, came debter for my sake,
So him I loose through my vnkinde abuse.
    Him haue I lost, thou hast both him and me,
    He paies the whole, and yet am I not free.

135

WHo euer hath her wish, thou hast thy *Will*,
    And *Will* too boote, and *Will* in ouer-plus,
More then enough am I that vexe thee still,
To thy sweet will making addition thus.
Wilt thou whose will is large and spatious,
Not once vouchsafe to hide my will in thine,
Shall will in others seeme right gracious,
And in my will no faire acceptance shine:
The sea all water, yet receiues raine still,
And in aboundance addeth to his store,
So thou beeing rich in *Will* adde to thy *Will*,
One will of mine to make thy large *Will* more.
    Let no vnkinde, no faire beseechers kill,
    Thinke all but one, and me in that one *Will*.

136

IF thy soule check thee that I come so neere,
    Sweare to thy blind soule that I was thy *Will*,
And will thy soule knowes is admitted there,
Thus farre for loue, my loue-sute sweet fullfill.
Will, will fulfill the treasure of thy loue,
I fill it full with wils, and my will one,
In things of great receit with ease we prooue,
Among a number one is reckon'd none.
Then in the number let me passe vntold,
Though in thy stores account I one must be,
For nothing hold me, so it please thee hold,
That nothing me, a some-thing sweet to thee.
    Make but my name thy loue, and loue that still,
    And then thou louest me for my name is *Will*.

137

THou blinde foole loue, what doost thou to mine eyes,

I   That

Sir John Gilbert Shakespeare's Plays, 1849

William Edward Frost, The Disarming of
Cupid, 1850 (for sonnet 154)

Of Mr. *William Shakespeare.*

What, lofty *Shakespeare*, art againe reviv'd?
And *Vertue* like now show'it thy felfe reviv'd,
'Tis love that thus to thee is showne.
The labours his, the glory ftil thine owne.
Thefe learned Poems amongft thine after-birth,
That makes thy name immortall on the earth,
Will make the learned ftill admire to fee,
The Mufes gifts fo fully infus'd on thee,
Let Carping *Momus* barke and bite his fill,
And ignorant *Davus* flight thy learned skill;
Yet thofe who know the worth of thy defert,
And with true judgement can difcerne thy Art,
Will be admirers of thy heh tun'd ftraine,
Amongft whofe number let me ftill remaine.

John Warren

POEMS:
VVRITTEN
BY
WIL. SHAKE-SPEARE.
Gent.

Printed at *London* by *Tho. Cotes*, and are
to be fold by *Iohn Benfon*, dwelling in
S[t]. *Dunftans* Church-yard.

1640 edition

John Henry Fuseli, Hamlet, Act I, Scene IV

Frank Howard, Portia Pronouncing Sentence,
c. 1830-1831

Illustration for A Lover's Complaint, 1774

Odilon Redon, Ophelia Among the Flowers, 1905

John William Waterhouse, 'Gather Ye Rosebuds' or 'Ophelia', 1908

A NOTE ON WILLIAM SHAKESPEARE'S POETRY

by Mark Tuley

The *Sonnets* are central to William Shakespeare's art. They display Shakespeare's poetic talent at its height. The *Sonnets* are the great love poem sequence in British poetry, as well as being the longest single group of English Renaissance sonnets. They rival in grandeur, skill and cleverness the poetic sequence from which they ultimately derive (via Sir Thomas Wyatt): Francesco Petrarch's *Rime Sparse*. In Shakespeare's art, introspection and self-analysis is as rigorous as in Petrarch's *Canzoniere*, but Shakespeare's bitterness and sense of irony is more deeply ingrained than in Petrarch's work.

William Shakespeare's *Sonnets* came late in the development of the Petrarchan sonnet sequence. They are decadent, late efforts of an already (by the 1590s) old-fashioned poetic form. Yet Shakespeare manages to infuse the form with an extraordinary power and magic. The *Sonnets*, indeed, contain some of the most marvellous moments in any (English) poetry. The magnificence of the opening lines of the *Sonnets*, for instance, is undeniable:

Shall I compare thee to a summer's day? (18.1)

Full many a glorious morning have I seen

Flatter the mountain tops with sovereign eye,
Kissing with golden face the meadows green,
Gilding pale streams with heavenly alchemy (33.1-4)

Take all my loves, my love, yea, take them all (40.1)

Sweet love, renew thy force (56.1)

Let me not to the marriage of true minds
Admit impediments: love is not love
Which alters when it alteration finds,
Or bends with the remover to remove. (116.1-4)

My love is as a fever, longing still (147.1)

Formally, William Shakespeare used the ordinary (British) sonnet rhyme scheme of abab, cdcd, efef, gg, 4 + 4 + 4 + 2, a pattern made popular by the Earl of Surrey in Tottel's *Miscellany*. The Surrey sonnet form, like Sir Thomas Wyatt's model (abba, abba, cddc, ee), was easier for English poets to use than the Petrarchan form of abab, abab, cde, cde. Shakespeare never employs the Italian sestet, the octave abba, cddc, and never crossed the 'turn' of the sonnet, between the octave and the sestet (except in the list poem, and in sonnet 148). The octave and the sestet were nearly always kept apart. He kept a distinct statement in each quatrain and the couplet. The couplet was nearly always a separate syntactical unit.

For all his other innovations, in the *Sonnets* William Shakespeare is formally uninventive and conservative, preferring to stick to Surrey's rhyme scheme. Other writers surpassed him for inventiveness (Donne, Herbert, Milton, Spenser, Lock). Nearly of the *Sonnets* are regular; only two sonnets are irregular: sonnet 126 with its twelve lines, and the fifteen line sonnet 99. Sonnet 145 is in tetrameters. There are few sonnets that are *not* addressed to the beloved; there are no dialogue sonnets, many puns and convoluted metaphors, but no word games such as acrostics, tails, anagrams or reversible lines. There are no dialogues with other poets, either British or European. None of Shakespeare's *Sonnets* has been translated or adapted from another source (as Sir Thomas Wyatt had done so skillfully with Petrarch).

Yet, despite his formal conservatism, William Shakespeare's *Sonnets* are without doubt the finest sonnet sequence in English, surpassing Edmund Spenser's *Amoretti*, Michael Drayton's *Idea* or Sir Philip Sidney's *Astrophil and Stella*. The Bard's ability to create word magic remains undiminished, even after centuries of quotation and discussion. It is the same with the plays – most obviously *Hamlet*, which seems to have a quotation or the title of a subsequent work of art (play, film, book) in every line.

•

The sexual situations and feelings evoked in the *Sonnets* chime with some of the more erotic moments from William Shakespeare's verse and plays, such as Venus's talk of 'sweet bottom-grass' (pubic hair) in *Venus and Adonis*, a bawdy word-play which chimes with the 'dark lady' sonnets (such as sonnet 135, one of the 'will' sonnets); or Berowne's Neoplatonic effusions from *Love's Labour's Lost*; or Feste's wistful song 'O mistress mine' in *Twelfth Night*; or Lady Macbeth's famous (and, for some, bewildering) exhortation 'unsex me here', a mysterious utterance, as ambiguous as the *Sonnets'* 'your eye I eyed'; or Juliet's more understandable urging in her 'Come, night; come, Romeo; come' speech. Juliet's 'come, Romeo' statement is a relatively straight-forward expression of erotic desire. Many Elizabethan poems begin thus:

'To come to thee, and be thy love, wrote Sir Walter Raleigh in 'The Nymph's Reply to the Shepherd';

'Come away, come, sweet love', urged an anonymous poem of 1597;

'Come, Night, and lay thy velvet hand

On glorious Day's outfacing face', wrote George Chapman in 'Epithalamion Teratos';

'Come away with me, and be my love', says Christopher Marlowe in 'The Passionate Shepherd to His Love';

'Come away, come away, my darling', urged Thomas Campion in "What then is love but mourning?";

and Ben Jonson wrote in 'To Celia': 'Come my Celia, let us prove'.

There is much ambiguity and confusion as to what or whom the incidents in the *Sonnets* refer to: no definite historical person or allusion in the *Sonnets* has been authoritatively confirmed. No date has been agreed upon for the creation of the *Sonnets* (critics have suggested dates between 1583 and 1609). There are no links that have been definitively established between William Shakespeare and Thorpe's quarto book. It is not certain whether Shakespeare planned the poems as a complete sequence, whether he ordered them as they were printed, whether he intended them to be printed like that, or whether he proof-read them; nor is it sure how Shakespeare regarded the *Sonnets* in relation to his plays and to *A Lover's Complaint*, nor how he intended them to be perceived.

It would have been no trouble at all for William Shakespeare to invent the situation of the *Sonnets*, with the narrator attracted to both the 'dark lady' and the young man. After all, Shakespeare also invented the self-tormented figure of Hamlet, one of the key psychological characters of the West (along with Oedipus and Faust). Shakespeare was the inventor of rapturous and wistful crossdressing and gender-play (*As You Like It* and *Twelfth Night*); the imagery of an old king descending into madness and berating the womb as a sulphurous pit (*King Lear*); a would-be monarch murdering his friend and imagining a knife and a ghost coming to haunt him (*Macbeth*); an exiled magician living on a witch's island controlling fairies and sprites (*The Tempest*).

William Shakespeare could conjure up scenes, like a magician, with a few words. The sexual triangle of the *Sonnets* would have presented him no problems at all. Easy for such a multi-talented writer to have the narrator attracted to both people, veering between love and hate, desire and self-loathing, discussing rivalry in art and love, the anxieties of patronage and class difference (between the narrator and the young man), and all the while being acutely, painfully aware of the passing of time.

Following selections from William Shakespeare's *Sonnets* and his poetry, I have included some famous passages from the plays. The book ends with some magical incantations, such as Propsero describing his 'rough magic', which 'op'd graves', or Puck's 'Now the hungry lion roars' speech, or Lear's bombast against the storm. These shamanic volleys, the highpoints of Shakespeare's own 'rough magic', fit in well with Lady Macbeth's 'Come, you spirits' monologue. To counter these visionary speeches, the 'What a piece of work is a man!', from *Hamlet* and 'Tomorrow and tomorrow and tomorrow' from *Macbeth* seem appropriate.

BIBLIOGRAPHY

William Shakespeare

The Sonnets, ed. Stephen Booth, Yale University Press, New Haven, 1978
The Sonnets, ed. Martin Seymour-Smith, Heinemann, 1963
The Sonnets, ed. Tucker Brooke, Oxford University Press, New York, 1936
Shakespeare's Sonnets, ed. W.G. Ingram & T. Redpath, Hodder & Stoughton, 1978

On William Shakespeare's *Sonnets*

G. Akrigg. *Shakespeare and the Earl of Southampton*, Hamish Hamilton, 1968
Michael J.B. Allen. "Shakespeare's Man Descending a Staircase: Sonnets 126-154", *Shakespeare Survey*, 31, 1978
Sandra Berman. *The Sonnet Over Time*, Chapel Hill, 1988
Harold Bloom, ed. *Shakespeare's Sonnets*, Chelsea House, New York, 1987
S. Booth. *An Essay on Shakespeare's Sonnets*, Yale University Press, New Haven, CT, 1969
Samuel Butler. *Shakespeare's Sonnets Reconsidered*, Cape, 1927
H. Calvert. *Shakespeare's Sonnets and the Problem of Autobiography*, Merlin Books, Brauton, Devon, 1987
S.C. Campbell. *Only Begotten Sonnets: A Reconstruction of Shakespeare's Sonnets Sequence*, Bell & Hyman, 1978
Reed Way Dasenbrock. *Imitating the Italians: Wyatt, Spenser, Syne, Pound, Joyce*, John Hopkins University Press, Baltimore, 1991
Denis Donoghue. "Shakespeare at Sonnets", *Swannee Review*, 88, 1980
Heather Dubrow. *Captive Victors: Shakespeare's Narrative Poems and Sonnets*, Cornell University Press, Ithaca, 1987
—. *Echoes of Desire: English Petrarchism and Its Counterdiscourses*, Cornell

University Press, 1995

Maurice Evans, ed. *Elizabethan Sonnets*, Dent, 1977

Margaret Ferguson. *Trials of Desire: Renaissance Defenses of Poetry*, Yale University Press, New Haven, 1983

—. *et al*, eds. *Rewriting the Renaissance*, University of Chicago Press, 1986

Anne Ferry. *The "Inward" Language: Sonnets of Wyatt, Sidney, Shakespeare, Donne*, University of Chicago Press, 1983

Joel Fineman. *Shakespeare's Perjured Eye: The Invention of Poetic Subjectivity in the Sonnets*, University of California Press, 1988

—. *The Subjectivity Effect in Western Literary Tradition: Essays Towards the Release of Shakespeare's Will*, MIT Press, Cambridge, Mass., 1991

M.B. Friedman. "Shakespeare's 'Master Mistris': Image and Tone in Sonnet 20", *Shakespeare Quarterly*, XXII, 2, Spring, 1971

R. Giroux. *The Book Known as Q: A Consideration of Shakespeare's Sonnets*, Weidenfeld & Nicholson, 1982

Andrew Gurr. "Shakespeare's First Poem: Sonnet 145", *Essays in Criticism*, 21, 1971

Gerald Hammond. *The Reader and Shakespeare's Young Man Sonnets*, Barnes & Noble, Totowa, New Jersey, 1981

Jane Hedley. *Power in Verse: Metaphor and Metonymy in the Renaiss-ance Lyric*, Pennsylvania State University Press, University Park, 1988

G. Hiller, ed. *Poems of the Elizabethan Age*, Methuen, 1977

James Hutton. "Analogues of Shakespeare's Sonnets 153-4: Contributions to the History of a Theme", *Modern Philology*, 38, 1940

Edward Hubler. *The Sense of Shakespeare's Sonnets*, Hill & Wang, New York, 1962

R. Jakobson & L.G. Jones. *Shakespeare's Verbal Art in 'The Expense of Spirit'*, Mouton, The Hague, 1970

P. Jones, ed. *Shakespeare: The Sonnets*, Macmillan, 1977

J. Kristeva. *Tales of Love*, tr Leon S. Roudiez, Columbia University Press, New York, 1987

Hilton Landry, ed. *New Essays on Shakespeare's Sonnets*, AMS Press, New York, 1976

—. *Interpretation in Shakespeare's Sonnets*, University of California Press, Berkeley, 1963

J.B. Leishman. *Themes and Variations in Shakespeare's Sonnets*, Hillary House, New York, 1963

J.W. Lever. *The Elizabethan Love Sonnet*, Methuen, 1956

Richard Levin. "Sonnet CXXIX as a 'Dramatic Poem'", *Shakespeare Quarterly*, 16, 1965

—. "Feminist Thematics and Shakespearean Tragedy", *PMLA*, 103, 1988

—. "The Poetics and Politics of Bardicide", *PMLA*, 105, 1990

Arthur Marotti. ""Love is not love": Elizabethan Sonnet Sequences and the Social Order", *English Literary History*, 49, 1982

Kenneth Muir. *Shakespeare's Sonnets*, Allen & Unwin, 1979

SELECTED POEMS ✢ 85

J. Padel. *New Poems by Shakespeare: Order and Meaning Restored to the Sonnets*, Herbert Press, 1981

Joseph Pequigney. *Such Is My Love: A Study of Shakespeare's Sonnets*, University of Chicago Press, 1985

Paul Ramsey. *The Fickle Glass: A Study of Shakespeare's Sonnets*, AMS Press, New York, 1979

H. Richmond. *Shakespeare's Sexual Comedy*, Bobbs, Indianapolis, 1971

G.M. Ridden. *Shakespeare's Sonnets*, Longman, 1982

A.L. Rowse. *Shakespeare's Sonnets*, Macmillan, 1964

—. *Shakespeare's Sonnets: The Problems Solved*, Harper & Row, New York, 1973

In the Dim Void

Samuel Beckett's Late Trilogy:
Company, Ill Seen, Ill Said and *Worstward Ho*

by Gregory Johns

This book discusses the luminous beauty and dense, rigorous poetry of Samuel Beckett's late works, *Company, Ill Seen, Ill Said* and *Worstward Ho*. Gregory Johns looks back over Beckett's long writing career, charting the development from the *Molloy-Malone Dies-Unnamable* trilogy through the 'fizzles' of the 1960s to the elegiac lyricism of the *Company* series. Johns compares the trilogy with late plays such as *Ghosts, Footfalls* and *Rockaby*.

Bibliography, notes. Illustrated. 120pp
ISBN 9781861712974 Pbk and ISBN 9781861712608 Hbk
9781861713407 E-book

ANDREI
TARKOVSKY

JEREMY MARK ROBINSON

POCKET GUIDE

Andrei Tarkovsky is one of the great filmmakers of recent times.

This book covers every aspect of Tarkovsky s artistic career, and all of his output, concentrating on his seven feature films: *Ivan's Childhood*, *Andrei Roublyov*, *Solaris*, *Mirror*, *Stalker*, *Nostalghia* and *The Sacrifice*, made between 1962 and 1986.

Part One of this study focusses on the key elements and themes of Andrei Tarkovsky's art: spirituality; childhood; the film image; poetics; painting and the history of art; the family; eroticism; symbolism; as well as technical areas, such as script, camera, sound, music, editing, budget and production.

Part Two explores Tarkovsky's films in detail, with scene-by-scene analyses (in some cases, shot-by-shot). Tarkovsky emerges as a brilliant, difficult, complex and poetic artist.

Fully illustrated. This new edition has been revised and updated.
ISBN 19781861713957 Pbk   9781861713834 Hbk

Beauties, Beasts, and Enchantment

CLASSIC FRENCH FAIRY TALES

Translated and with an Introduction
by Jack Zipes

A collection of 36 classic French fairy tales translated by renowned writer Jack Zipes.
Cinderella, Beauty and the Beast, Sleeping Beauty and *Little Red Riding Hood* are among the
classic fairy tales in this amazing book.
Includes illustrations from fairy tale collections.
Jack Zipes has written and published widely on fairy tales.

'Terrific... a succulent array of 17th and 18th century 'salon' fairy tales'
- *The New York Times Book Review*

'These tales are adventurous, thrilling in a way fairy tales are meant to be... The translation
from the French is modern, happily free of archaic and hyperbolic language... a fine and
sophisticated collection' - *New York Tribune*

'Enjoyable to read... a unique collection of French regional folklore' - *Library Journal*

'Charming stories accompanied by attractive pen-and-ink drawings' - *Chattanooga Times*

Introduction and illustrations 612pp. ISBN 9781861712510 Pbk ISBN 9781861713193 Hbk

CRESCENT MOON PUBLISHING

web: www.crmoon.com e-mail: cresmopub@yahoo.co.uk

ARTS, PAINTING, SCULPTURE

The Art of Andy Goldsworthy
Andy Goldsworthy: Touching Nature
Andy Goldsworthy in Close-Up
Andy Goldsworthy: Pocket Guide
Andy Goldsworthy In America
Land Art: A Complete Guide
The Art of Richard Long
Richard Long: Pocket Guide
Land Art In the UK
Land Art in Close-Up
Land Art In the U.S.A.
Land Art: Pocket Guide
Installation Art in Close-Up
Minimal Art and Artists In the 1960s and After
Colourfield Painting
Land Art DVD, TV documentary
Andy Goldsworthy DVD, TV documentary
The Erotic Object: Sexuality in Sculpture From Prehistory to the Present Day
Sex in Art: Pornography and Pleasure in Painting and Sculpture
Postwar Art
Sacred Gardens: The Garden in Myth, Religion and Art
Glorification: Religious Abstraction in Renaissance and 20th Century Art
Early Netherlandish Painting
Leonardo da Vinci
Piero della Francesca
Giovanni Bellini
Fra Angelico: Art and Religion in the Renaissance
Mark Rothko: The Art of Transcendence
Frank Stella: American Abstract Artist
Jasper Johns
Brice Marden
Alison Wilding: The Embrace of Sculpture
Vincent van Gogh: Visionary Landscapes
Eric Gill: Nuptials of God
Constantin Brancusi: Sculpting the Essence of Things
Max Beckmann
Caravaggio
Gustave Moreau
Egon Schiele: Sex and Death In Purple Stockings
Delizioso Fotografico Fervore: Works In Process 1
Sacro Cuore: Works In Process 2
The Light Eternal: J.M.W. Turner
The Madonna Glorified: Karen Arthurs

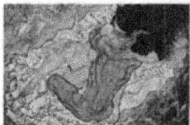

LITERATURE

J.R.R. Tolkien: The Books, The Films, The Whole Cultural Phenomenon
J.R.R. Tolkien: Pocket Guide
Tolkien's Heroic Quest
The *Earthsea* Books of Ursula Le Guin
Beauties, Beasts and Enchantment: Classic French Fairy Tales
German Popular Stories by the Brothers Grimm
Philip Pullman and *His Dark Materials*
Sexing Hardy: Thomas Hardy and Feminism
Thomas Hardy's *Tess of the d'Urbervilles*
Thomas Hardy's *Jude the Obscure*
Thomas Hardy: The Tragic Novels
Love and Tragedy: Thomas Hardy
The Poetry of Landscape in Hardy
Wessex Revisited: Thomas Hardy and John Cowper Powys
Wolfgang Iser: Essays and Interviews
Petrarch, Dante and the Troubadours
Maurice Sendak and the Art of Children's Book Illustration
Andrea Dworkin
Cixous, Irigaray, Kristeva: The *Jouissance* of French Feminism
Julia Kristeva: Art, Love, Melancholy, Philosophy, Semiotics and Psychoanalysis
Hélene Cixous I Love You: The *Jouissance* of Writing
Luce Irigaray: Lips, Kissing, and the Politics of Sexual Difference
Peter Redgrove: Here Comes the Flood
Peter Redgrove: Sex-Magic-Poetry-Cornwall
Lawrence Durrell: Between Love and Death, East and West
Love, Culture & Poetry: Lawrence Durrell
Cavafy: Anatomy of a Soul
German Romantic Poetry: Goethe, Novalis, Heine, Hölderlin
Feminism and Shakespeare
Shakespeare: Love, Poetry & Magic
The Passion of D.H. Lawrence
D.H. Lawrence: Symbolic Landscapes
D.H. Lawrence: Infinite Sensual Violence
Rimbaud: Arthur Rimbaud and the Magic of Poetry
The Ecstasies of John Cowper Powys
Sensualism and Mythology: The Wessex Novels of John Cowper Powys
Amorous Life: John Cowper Powys and the Manifestation of Affectivity (H.W. Fawkner)
Postmodern Powys: New Essays on John Cowper Powys (Joe Boulter)
Rethinking Powys: Critical Essays on John Cowper Powys
Paul Bowles & Bernardo Bertolucci
Rainer Maria Rilke
Joseph Conrad: *Heart of Darkness*
In the Dim Void: Samuel Beckett
Samuel Beckett Goes into the Silence
André Gide: Fiction and Fervour
Jackie Collins and the Blockbuster Novel
Blinded By Her Light: The Love-Poetry of Robert Graves
The Passion of Colours: Travels In Mediterranean Lands
Poetic Forms

POETRY

Ursula Le Guin: Walking In Cornwall
Peter Redgrove: Here Comes The Flood
Peter Redgrove: Sex-Magic-Poetry-Cornwall
Dante: Selections From the Vita Nuova
Petrarch, Dante and the Troubadours
William Shakespeare: Sonnets
William Shakespeare: Complete Poems
Blinded By Her Light: The Love-Poetry of Robert Graves
Emily Dickinson: Selected Poems
Emily Brontë: Poems
Thomas Hardy: Selected Poems
Percy Bysshe Shelley: Poems
John Keats: Selected Poems
Joh n Keats: Poems of 1820
D.H. Lawrence: Selected Poems
Edmund Spenser: Poems
Edmund Spenser: Amoretti
John Donne: Poems
Henry Vaughan: Poems
Sir Thomas Wyatt: Poems
Robert Herrick: Selected Poems
Rilke: Space, Essence and Angels in the Poetry of Rainer Maria Rilke
Rainer Maria Rilke: Selected Poems
Friedrich Hölderlin: Selected Poems
Arseny Tarkovsky: Selected Poems
Arthur Rimbaud: Selected Poems
Arthur Rimbaud: A Season in Hell
Arthur Rimbaud and the Magic of Poetry
Novalis: Hymns To the Night
German Romantic Poetry
Paul Verlaine: Selected Poems
Elizaethan Sonnet Cycles
D.J. Enright: By-Blows
Jeremy Reed: Brigitte's Blue Heart
Jeremy Reed: Claudia Schiffer's Red Shoes
Gorgeous Little Orpheus
Radiance: New Poems
Crescent Moon Book of Nature Poetry
Crescent Moon Book of Love Poetry
Crescent Moon Book of Mystical Poetry
Crescent Moon Book of Elizabethan Love Poetry
Crescent Moon Book of Metaphysical Poetry
Crescent Moon Book of Romantic Poetry
Pagan America: New American Poetry

MEDIA, CINEMA, FEMINISM and CULTURAL STUDIES

J.R.R. Tolkien: The Books, The Films, The Whole Cultural Phenomenon
J.R.R. Tolkien: Pocket Guide
The *Lord of the Rings* Movies: Pocket Guide
The Cinema of Hayao Miyazaki
Hayao Miyazaki: *Princess Mononoke*: Pocket Movie Guide
Hayao Miyazaki: *Spirited Away*: Pocket Movie Guide
Tim Burton : Hallowe'en For Hollywood
Ken Russell
Ken Russell: *Tommy*: Pocket Movie Guide
The Ghost Dance: The Origins of Religion
The Peyote Cult
Cixous, Irigaray, Kristeva: The *Jouissance* of French Feminism
Julia Kristeva: Art, Love, Melancholy, Philosophy, Semiotics and Psychoanalysis
Luce Irigaray: Lips, Kissing, and the Politics of Sexual Difference
Hélene Cixous I Love You: The *Jouissance* of Writing
Andrea Dworkin
'Cosmo Woman': The World of Women's Magazines
Women in Pop Music
HomeGround: The Kate Bush Anthology
Discovering the Goddess (Geoffrey Ashe)
The Poetry of Cinema
The Sacred Cinema of Andrei Tarkovsky
Andrei Tarkovsky: Pocket Guide
Andrei Tarkovsky: *Mirror*: Pocket Movie Guide
Andrei Tarkovsky: *The Sacrifice*: Pocket Movie Guide
Walerian Borowczyk: Cinema of Erotic Dreams
Jean-Luc Godard: The Passion of Cinema
Jean-Luc Godard: *Hail Mary*: Pocket Movie Guide
Jean-Luc Godard: *Contempt*: Pocket Movie Guide
Jean-Luc Godard: *Pierrot le Fou*: Pocket Movie Guide
John Hughes and Eighties Cinema
Ferris Bueller's Day Off: Pocket Movie Guide
Jean-Luc Godard: Pocket Guide
The Cinema of Richard Linklater
Liv Tyler: Star In Ascendance
Blade Runner and the Films of Philip K. Dick
Paul Bowles and Bernardo Bertolucci
Media Hell: Radio, TV and the Press
An Open Letter to the BBC
Detonation Britain: Nuclear War in the UK
Feminism and Shakespeare
Wild Zones: Pornography, Art and Feminism
Sex in Art: Pornography and Pleasure in Painting and Sculpture
Sexing Hardy: Thomas Hardy and Feminism

The Light Eternal is a model monograph, an exemplary job. The subject matter of the book is beautifully
organised and dead on beam. (Lawrence Durrell)
It is amazing for me to see my work treated with such passion and respect. (Andrea Dworkin)

CRESCENT MOON PUBLISHING
P.O. Box 1312, Maidstone, Kent, ME14 5XU, Great Britain. www.crmoon.com

cresmopub@yahoo.co.uk   www.crescentmoon.org.uk

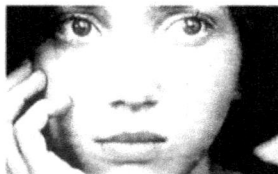